HEALTH FOR LIFE

diabetes 2

JODY VASSALLO

WHAT IS DIABETES?

Diabetes is a condition where there is too much sugar (glucose) in the blood because the body cannot produce enough insulin or use it properly. When we eat food that contains carbohydrate, the level of glucose (sugar) in the blood rises as the carbohydrate is digested into glucose and absorbed into the blood. In healthy people, the rise in blood glucose stimulates the pancreas to release the hormone insulin, which allows body cells to absorb the glucose and fats in the blood, causing the blood glucose level to return to normal. Due to the lack of effective insulin in people with diabetes, blood glucose rises to a higher level after eating, doesn't fall as quickly, and remains higher than normal hours after eating. If not treated, the high blood glucose and fat levels can damage eyes, nerves and blood vessels, and increase the risk of heart disease, kidney and circulatory problems. Symptoms of undiagnosed diabetes include frequent urination, excessive thirst, tiredness, infections and blurred vision. Early diagnosis and treatment are essential to minimise the risk of serious health problems.

TYPES OF DIABETES

There are three main types of diabetes. People with **Type 1** (insulin-dependent or juvenile-onset) diabetes cannot make the hormone insulin in their pancreas and require daily insulin injections. **Type 2** (non-insulin dependent or adult-onset) diabetes is the most common and usually develops in overweight, middle-aged people when their body can't make enough insulin or respond to it properly (insulin resistance).

Gestational diabetes is a temporary form that can develop during pregnancy. Impaired glucose tolerance is a pre-diabetic condition, where blood glucose is higher than normal but not in the diabetic range.

MANAGING DIABETES

The main treatment goal for any type of diabetes is to keep the blood glucose level as close to normal as possible. Improved food choices and regular exercise are both very important for achieving this. There is no one ideal diabetic diet, because people with diabetes have different nutritional needs depending on their age, lifestyle and physical condition, but there are basic principles for healthy eating for people with diabetes:

1 | **Eat a variety of foods at each meal**
2 | **Eat regular meals based on low-GI, carbohydrate-rich foods**
3 | **Limit your saturate fat consumption and have a moderate total fat intake**
4 | **Eat more fresh vegetables and fruit and legumes**
5 | **Eat more fibre**
6 | **Limit your intake of added sugars**
7 | **Limit your salt intake**
8 | **Only drink alcohol in moderation, if at all.**

This book is designed to provide general guidelines for healthy eating for people with diabetes, and the recipes are designed to help you meet these goals. The recipes and guidelines are also applicable to people without diabetes, who are also at risk of developing heart disease and diabetes.

Dr Susanna Holt (PhD, dietitian)

THE GLYCAEMIC INDEX

Different foods contain different types of carbohydrates (starches and sugars), which vary in their size and physical form. Some carbohydrates are digested or broken down into glucose at a relatively fast rate and cause a rapid, large rise in blood glucose, which is more pronounced in those with diabetes. Other carbohydrates are digested at a slower rate and cause a smaller, more gradual rise in blood glucose. The way foods are prepared and cooked also affects the rate at which the food's carbohydrate is digested. For example, soft, soggy pasta that was cooked for a long time is more quickly digested than harder pasta that was cooked for a shorter time.

Scientists developed the glycaemic index (GI) method to measure the extent to which equal-carbohydrate portions of different foods increase blood glucose after being eaten. Even though they contain the same amounts of carbohydrate, foods with a high GI value (70 or more) are digested more quickly and produce a faster and higher rise in blood sugar than foods with a medium (56 to 69) or low GI value (55 or less), which are more slowly digested. Due to their lower blood glucose response, low-GI foods require less insulin in order to be metabolised. Whenever possible, people with diabetes should choose carbohydrate-rich foods with low to medium GI values. Scientific research has shown that a diet based on low-GI carbohydrate-rich foods can improve blood glucose control, lower blood cholesterol, assist with weight loss and reduce the risk of heart disease.

TIPS FOR LOW-GI EATING

| Swap light, fluffy breakfast cereals with high-fibre varieties and traditional porridge.
| Add milk and/or fresh fruit to breakfast cereal to reduce the blood glucose response to the cereal.
| Choose denser breads containing whole or cracked grains, and those made from stone-ground flours.
| Add barley or lentils to rice to lower the overall GI and reduce the amount of rice you eat.
| Instead of potatoes, use legumes, pasta, low-GI noodles, steamed unpeeled orange sweet potato, basmati rice or Doongara rice (CleverRice™).
| Don't chop or cut foods too finely or puree or mash them (this increases their GI value).
| Add a green salad dressed with vinegar to meals containing starchy foods, such as rice or potatoes (the vinegar helps reduce the meal's GI value).
| In place of potatoes and swedes, add pasta and legumes (such as lentils, beans, split peas) to soups and casseroles.
| Don't cook pasta or rice until it is soft and soggy.
| Serve pasta with lots of salad and a tomato-based sauce, so you can fill up on vegetables and reduce the amount of pasta you eat.
| Add some lean protein and/or healthy fat to a carbohydrate-rich meal to help slow digestion and prevent blood glucose from rising too high (eg, eating grainy toast with ricotta cheese or avocado and tomato, or serving pasta with salmon and tomato sauce—but treat fat with care if you're watching your weight).

GI SYMBOL ON FOOD LABELS

If foods and drinks display the GI symbol, they have had their GI value measured accurately and must meet other healthy eating guidelines (low in saturated fat, low to moderate salt content, contain at least 10 grams of carbohydrate per serve). They must also have their GI value listed near the nutrition information panel. The GI symbol program is run by a non-profit organisation called Glycemic Index Ltd.

ABOUT THE RECIPES

Underneath each recipe, you will find the approximate nutrient content of an average-sized portion of the finished dish and an estimated GI value. The GI values are estimates only and were calculated using published GI values for each of the carbohydrate-containing ingredients in the recipe. If an ingredient didn't have a published GI value, the GI value of the most similar foodstuff was used as a substitute. For this reason, and the fact that food preparation and cooking methods can affect a food's GI value, it is not possible to precisely estimate the GI value of a recipe, but it's likely that the recipe's GI category (low, medium or high) will be correctly estimated. Consequently, people with diabetes should measure their own blood glucose responses to the recipes in order to find the meals that give them the lowest blood glucose responses.

Each recipe's estimated GI rating is based on the weighted GI values of each ingredient and was calculated by an experienced dietitian using the following steps:
1 | Work out the total amount of carbohydrate in the recipe.
2 | Calculate the percentage of total carbohydrate provided by each ingredient.
3 | For each ingredient, multiply the ingredient's GI value by the percentage carbohydrate it provides (from step 2).
4 | Add up the values calculated in step 3 to obtain the estimated GI rating.

GLYCAEMIC LOAD

GI values for foods are measured for portions containing a certain amount of carbohydrate, usually 50 grams, as a way of comparing foods on the same relative basis (blood glucose response per 50 grams of carbohydrate). However, people eat portions of foods containing varying amounts of carbohydrate. Researchers have now come up with a new concept called 'the glycaemic load' (GL), which is a way of estimating the rise in blood glucose produced by any sized portion of a carbohydrate-rich food. A GL value is calculated for a specific amount of food by multiplying the carbohydrate in that amount of food by the food's GI value. In general, GL values won't matter if you simply eat low-GI foods instead of high-GI versions in similar amounts, because the low-GI foods won't cause your blood glucose to rise as high. You would need to use a blood glucose monitor to work out how GL values correspond to your own blood glucose measurements, and use this information to work out how much food you can eat.

THE GI GUIDE

Some easy ways to switch from high- to low-GI foods

HIGHER-GI	LOWER-GI ALTERNATIVE*
Breads & crackers White, fine wholemeal or rye bread ǀ puffed crispbreads ǀ water crackers ǀ thin savoury crackers ǀ puffed rice cakes ǀ rice crackers	Denser breads with whole or cracked grains or made from stone-ground flour ǀ pumpernickel ǀ sourdough ǀ fruit loaf ǀ Vita Weat and Ryvita crispbreads
Breakfast cereals Highly processed cereals ǀ puffed rice or wheat ǀ corn flakes ǀ wheat flakes ǀ plain wheat biscuits ǀ bran flakes ǀ shredded wheat	Extruded bran cereals (All Bran, Ultra Bran, Soytana) ǀ psyllium fibre cereal (Guardian) ǀ porridge made from whole rolled oats or barley (not instant) ǀ natural muesli ǀ wheat biscuits with oat bran or soy and linseed
Grains Rice (Calrose, pelde, jasmine, glutinous, white arborio/risotto, instant) ǀ millet ǀ couscous	Rice (Doongara, basmati, wild) ǀ barley ǀ buckwheat ǀ burghul ǀ semolina
Pasta & noodles Gluten-free corn or rice pasta ǀ gnocchi ǀ cooked dried rice noodles ǀ udon noodles	Durum wheat pasta ǀ split pea and soy pasta ǀ meat-filled ravioli or tortellini ǀ fresh rice noodles ǀ mung bean noodles ǀ soba noodles
Starchy vegetables & legumes Potatoes ǀ parsnips ǀ swede ǀ pumpkin ǀ tapioca ǀ broad beans ǀ beetroot	All types of legumes (soya beans, lentils, chickpeas, kidney beans etc) ǀ sweet potato ǀ yam ǀ taro ǀ cassava ǀ corn ǀ green peas ǀ carrots
Fruit Lychees ǀ pineapple ǀ watermelon ǀ raisins ǀ rockmelon ǀ pawpaw ǀ very ripe bananas ǀ breadfruit ǀ dried dates ǀ dark red cherries	Apples ǀ pears ǀ citrus fruit ǀ plums ǀ peaches ǀ prunes ǀ berries ǀ custard apple ǀ apricots
Dairy products & alternatives Sweetened condensed milk ǀ some ice creams	Cow's milk ǀ soy milk ǀ yoghurt ǀ custard ǀ most ice creams (choose low-fat types)

* People with diabetes should monitor their individual blood glucose responses to these foods, as some people will produce higher blood glucose responses than others to the same foods.

Reference for foods in table: *The New Glucose Revolution*, Professor Jennie Brand-Miller, Kaye Foster-Powell and Dr Stephen Colagiuri. Published by Hodder Headline Australia Pty Ltd, Sydney, 2002. For additional information about GI values see: http://www.glycemicindex.com

INTRODUCTION 7

BREAKFAST

make at home muesli

MAKE AT HOME MUESLI

2 cups (200 g/6½ oz) raw rolled oats
2 cups (140 g/4½ oz) All-Bran® (processed wheat bran cereal)
2 cups (60 g/2 oz) Guardian® (wheat, psyllium, oat bran and barley cereal)
½ cup (70 g/2¼ oz) unprocessed oat bran
2 cups (180 g/6 oz) roughly chopped dried apple
1 cup (135 g/4½ oz) dried apricot halves, roughly chopped
1 cup (190 g/6¼ oz) dried pear, roughly chopped
1 cup (170 g/5⅔ oz) sultanas
½ cup (75 g/2½ oz) sunflower seeds
½ cup (70 g/2¼ oz) pepitas

1 Put all of the ingredients into a large bowl. Mix gently to combine.
2 Transfer the muesli to a large airtight container and seal until ready to use. Store in an airtight container for up to 1 month. Serve with reduced-fat milk.
Makes 12 cups
per cup | fat 8.5 g | protein 9 g | carbohydrate 56.5 g | fibre 12.5 g | cholesterol 0 mg | energy 1405 kJ (335 Cal) | gi 41 ▼ low*

*The GI will depend on the type of oats used. The coarser and less processed the oats, the lower the GI value.

H.E.L.T.

4 slices (180 g/6 oz) seeded wholegrain bread
100 g (3⅓ oz) sliced 97% fat-free ham
2 large ripe tomatoes, thickly sliced
canola oil spray
4 eggs
½ small iceberg lettuce, cut into wedges
1 tablespoon low-fat mayonnaise
cracked black pepper

1 Toast the bread and place on 4 serving plates. Divide the ham among the toast. Arrange the tomatoes on top of the ham.
2 Lightly spray a non-stick fry pan with canola oil spray. Heat the pan over medium heat. Crack the eggs into the pan and cook until done to your liking.
3 Place the eggs on top of the tomatoes, and the lettuce on the side. Drizzle the mayonnaise over the lettuce and sprinkle with cracked black pepper.
Serves 4
per serve | fat 9 g | protein 16.5 g | carbohydrate 22 g | fibre 4 g | cholesterol 201.5 mg | energy 990 kJ (235 Cal) | gi 46 ▼ low

h.e.l.t.

cheese & tomato french toast

CHEESE & TOMATO FRENCH TOAST

1 Cut the bread into four 2 cm (¾ in) thick slices. Using a serrated knife, cut a pocket through the center of each slice of bread, taking care not to cut all the way through. Season the tomatoes with cracked black pepper. Open the bread pocket slightly and slide a few slices of tomato into the center. Press together and seal with a toothpick.
2 Whisk the egg whites and season with cracked black pepper. Dip the bread, one slice at a time, into the egg mixture, then gently press into the parmesan to coat each side.
3 Melt the margarine in a non-stick fry pan over medium heat. Cook the bread until the egg has set and the parmesan is crisp and golden on both sides.
4 Cut each slice of toast in half. Serve with the rocket to the side. Serves 4

per serve | fat 6.5 g | protein 14 g | carbohydrate 36 g | fibre 5 g | cholesterol 8.5 mg | energy 1110 kJ (265 Cal) | gi 48 ▼ low

1 small loaf (320 g/10⅔ oz) day-old wholegrain bread
2 medium ripe tomatoes, sliced lengthwise
cracked black pepper
3 egg whites
⅓ cup (30 g/1 oz) finely grated parmesan cheese
10 g (⅓ oz) reduced-fat polyunsaturated margarine
50 g (1⅔ oz) baby rocket (arugula)

semolina with banana & nuts

SEMOLINA WITH BANANA & NUTS

1 Put the semolina and milk into a pan and stir over medium heat until the semolina is thick and soft.
2 Spoon the semolina into 4 serving bowls. Top with the yoghurt and bananas. Serve with the pistachios and honey. Serves 4
per serve | fat 6.5 g | protein 11.5 g | carbohydrate 33.5 g | fibre 2.5 g | cholesterol 6 mg | energy 1005 kJ (240 Cal) | gi 44 ▼ low

¼ cup (40 g/1⅓ oz) semolina
2½ cups (625 ml/20 fl oz) reduced-fat milk
100 g (3⅓ oz) low-fat plain yoghurt
2 medium bananas, sliced
50 g (1⅔ oz) pistachio kernels, roughly chopped
1 tablespoon yellow box honey

SUNRISE JUICE

1 Divide the passionfruit among 4 tall chilled glasses.
2 Put the strawberries into a blender and blend until smooth. Gently pour the puree over the passionfruit to form 2 separate layers.
3 Combine the pineapple juice and apple juice. Carefully pour over the puree. Serves 4
per serve | fat 0.2 g | protein 1.5 g | carbohydrate 30 g | fibre 3 g | cholesterol 0 mg | energy 520 kJ (125 Cal) | gi 41 ▼ low

¼ cup (60 ml/2 fl oz) passionfruit pulp
220 g (7 oz) strawberries, hulled
1 cup (250 ml/8 fl oz) unsweetened pineapple juice
3 cups (750 ml/24 fl oz) unsweetened apple juice

sunrise juice

mango, peach & papaya summer salad

MANGO, PEACH & PAPAYA SUMMER SALAD

2 mangoes, thickly sliced
3 medium peaches, unpeeled and cut into wedges
500 g (1 lb) red papaya, thickly sliced
2 teaspoons lime juice
2 tablespoons small fresh mint leaves
200 g (6½ oz) no-fat, no-added sugar vanilla yoghurt

1 Put the mangoes, peaches and papaya into a bowl. Mix gently to combine.
2 Drizzle the lime juice over the fruit mixture and sprinkle with the mint leaves.
3 Spoon the fruit mixture into 4 serving bowls. Serve with the yoghurt. Serves 4
per serve | fat 0.5 g | protein 5 g | carbohydrate 28 g | fibre 5.5 g | cholesterol 4 mg | energy 580 kJ (140 Cal) | gi 48 ▼ low

BANANA MALT SMOOTHIE

1 medium banana, roughly chopped
4 pitted prunes, roughly chopped
1 tablespoon malt milk powder
1 tablespoon rice bran
½ cup (125 g/4 oz) no-fat, no-added sugar vanilla yoghurt
2 cups (500 ml/16 fl oz) reduced-fat soy milk, chilled
ground nutmeg

1 Put the banana and prunes into a blender.
2 Add the milk powder, rice bran, yoghurt and soy milk. Blend until thick and creamy. Serve in large chilled mugs, sprinkled with a little nutmeg. Serves 2
per serve | fat 3 g | protein 15 g | carbohydrate 39 g | fibre 5 g | cholesterol 5.5 mg | energy 1015 kJ (240 Cal) | gi 41 ▼ low

banana malt smoothie

MEXICAN BEANS & EGGS

4 small (100 g/3⅓ oz) flour tortillas
canola oil spray
4 eggs
400 g (13 oz) can reduced-salt baked beans
2 teaspoons chopped bottled jalepeño peppers
2 tablespoons grated reduced-fat cheddar cheese

1 Wrap the tortillas in foil. Place them under a grill preheated to medium for 10 minutes or until they are warm. (Alternatively, follow the instructions on the packet and heat until warm in the microwave.)
2 Lightly spray a non-stick fry pan with canola oil spray. Heat the pan over medium heat. Crack the eggs into the pan and cook until done to your liking. Set aside and keep warm.
3 Put the baked beans and jalepeño peppers into a small pan. Cook over medium heat for 5 minutes or until heated through.
4 Arrange the tortillas in 4 small shallow heatproof bowls. Divide the beans among the bowls, top with an egg and sprinkle with a little grated cheese. Cook under the grill until the cheese is melted and bubbling. Serves 4

per serve | fat 9 g | protein 15.5 g | carbohydrate 24.5 g | fibre 5.5 g | cholesterol 192 mg | energy 1020 kJ (245 Cal) | gi 40 ▼ low

mexican beans & eggs

corn, spinach & chive omelette

CORN, SPINACH & CHIVE OMELETTE

1 Whisk the egg whites, chives, corn and spinach together. Season with cracked black pepper.
2 Lightly spray a non-stick fry pan with canola oil spray. Heat the pan over medium heat, add a quarter of the egg white mixture and swirl to coat the base of the pan.
3 Sprinkle with a quarter of the grated cheese. Cook for 3-5 minutes or until the underneath just begins to set. Fold in half using an egg slice. Slide onto a plate. Repeat with the remaining egg white mixture and grated cheese. Serve with wholegrain toast.
Serves 4
per serve | fat 2.5 g | protein 11 g | carbohydrate 6 g | fibre 1.5 g | cholesterol 6 mg | energy 380 kJ (90 Cal) | gi 55 ▼ low

8 egg whites
2 tablespoons snipped fresh chives
130 g (4½ oz) can creamed corn
50 g (1⅔ oz) baby spinach, roughly chopped
cracked black pepper
canola oil spray
⅓ cup (40 g/1⅓ oz) grated reduced-fat cheddar cheese

SPICED BIRCHER MUESLI

- 1 medium green apple, unpeeled and grated
- 1 medium pear, unpeeled and grated
- 1 cup (90 g/3 oz) roughly chopped dried apple
- 2 tablespoons sultanas
- ½ cup (125 g/4 oz) low-fat plain yoghurt
- ½ cup (125 g/4 oz) no-fat, no-added sugar vanilla yoghurt
- 1 teaspoon mixed spice
- 2 cups (200 g/6½ oz) raw rolled oats

1 Put the grated apple and pear into a large bowl.
2 Stir in the dried apple, sultanas, plain yoghurt, vanilla yoghurt and mixed spice.
3 Add the rolled oats and mix to combine. Divide the mixture among 4 serving bowls and serve immediately. Serves 4

per serve | fat 4.5 g | protein 10 g | carbohydrate 63.5 g | fibre 7.5 g | cholesterol 4 mg | energy 1400 kJ (335 Cal) | gi 44 ▼ low*

* The GI will depend on the type of oats used. The coarser and less processed the oats, the lower the GI value.

spiced bircher muesli

SOUPS & SNACKS

mango coconut yoghurt pops

MANGO COCONUT YOGHURT POPS

450 g (15 oz) fresh or canned mango flesh, roughly chopped
200 g (6½ oz) no-fat, no-added sugar vanilla yoghurt
1 tablespoon shredded coconut

1 Put the mango, yoghurt and coconut into a bowl and mix to combine. Divide the mixture among 8 x ⅓ cup (80 ml/2⅔ fl oz) capacity ice block moulds. Add the sticks and freeze overnight or until firm.
2 Rub a warm cloth over the outside of each ice block hole and gently pull the stick to remove. Makes 8

per yoghurt pop | fat 0.5 g | protein 2 g | carbohydrate 8.5 g | fibre 1 g | cholesterol 2 mg | energy 205 kJ (50 Cal) | gi 46 ▼ low

SPLIT PEA & CHICKEN SOUP

1.5 kg (3 lb) chicken, skin removed
1 medium onion, chopped
1 medium carrot, chopped
2 medium celery sticks, chopped
1 bay leaf
2 cups (420 g/14 oz) dried green split peas
10 cups (2.5 litres/80 fl oz) water
cracked black pepper

1 Put the chicken, onion, carrot, celery, bay leaf, split peas and water into a large pan. Bring to the boil, reduce the heat and simmer, covered, for 2 hours or until the split peas are soft.
2 Remove the chicken from the soup and cool slightly. Discard the bones and roughly shred the chicken meat.
3 Return the chicken to the pan and cook until heated through. Remove the bay leaf and season with cracked black pepper. Serves 6

per serve | fat 13 g | protein 53.5 g | carbohydrate 34.5 g | fibre 8 g | cholesterol 141 mg | energy 1950 kJ (465 Cal) | gi 31 ▼ low

split pea & chicken soup

smoked salmon pumpernickel

SMOKED SALMON PUMPERNICKEL

1 Place the capsicum under a grill preheated to high until the skin blisters and blackens. Transfer to a plastic bag to cool. Peel away and discard the skin, remove the seeds and cut the flesh into thin strips.
2 Put the capsicum, red onion, capers, smoked salmon, dill and lemon juice into a bowl. Mix gently to combine.
3 Cut the bread slices in half. Spoon the smoked salmon mixture on top and serve immediately. Serves 8 as a snack
per serve | fat 2 g | protein 9.5 g | carbohydrate 22.5 g | fibre 4.5 g | cholesterol 12 mg | energy 605 kJ (145 Cal) | gi 47 ▼ low

1 medium red capsicum (bell pepper)
1 medium red (Spanish) onion, thinly sliced
1 tablespoon capers, roughly chopped
200 g (6½ oz) smoked salmon, sliced
1 tablespoon chopped fresh dill
1 tablespoon lemon juice
8 slices (400 g/13 oz) pumpernickel bread

WHITE BEAN & SALSA SOUP

1 Heat the oil in a large pan, add the spring onions, garlic, cumin and coriander and cook over medium heat for 5 minutes or until the spring onions are soft.
2 Add the butter beans and stock, cover and cook for 15 minutes or until the beans are soft and heated through. Cool slightly before pureeing the soup in batches until smooth.
3 Return the soup to the cleaned pan and cook over medium heat until boiling. Cover and keep warm.
4 Put the avocado, extra spring onions, tomato, chilli, lime juice, paprika and extra virgin olive oil into a bowl and mix to combine.
5 Serve the soup in warmed bowls or mugs with a large spoonful of salsa on top. Serves 6
per serve | fat 13 g | protein 7 g | carbohydrate 7 g | fibre 5.5 g | cholesterol 0 mg | energy 710 kJ (170 Cal) | gi 21 ▼ low

2 teaspoons olive oil
6 spring onions (scallions), sliced
3 cloves garlic, crushed
½ teaspoon ground cumin
½ teaspoon ground coriander
1.6 kg (3 lb 3 oz) canned butter beans, rinsed and drained
3 cups (750 ml/24 fl oz) reduced-salt chicken stock
1 medium avocado, diced
2 spring onions (scallions), sliced, extra
1 medium tomato, diced
1 green chilli, finely chopped
1 tablespoon lime juice
½ teaspoon mild paprika
2 teaspoons extra virgin olive oil

white bean & salsa soup

red capsicum hummus

RED CAPSICUM HUMMUS

2 medium red capsicums (bell peppers)
400 g (13 oz) can chickpeas, rinsed and drained
1/3 cup (80 ml/2 2/3 fl oz) tahini
1/4 cup (60 ml/2 fl oz) lemon juice
3 cloves garlic
1/4 teaspoon cayenne pepper
1 teaspoon sweet paprika
1/2 teaspoon ground cumin

1 Place the capsicums under a grill preheated to high until the skin blisters and blackens. Transfer to a plastic bag to cool. Peel away and discard the skin, remove the seeds and roughly chop the flesh.
2 Put the capsicums, chickpeas, tahini, lemon juice, garlic and spices into a food processor and process to form a smooth creamy paste. Serve with pita crisps or vegetable crudités. Serves 10 as a snack
per serve | fat 5.5 g | protein 3.5 g | carbohydrate 4.5 g | fibre 2.5 g | cholesterol 0 mg | energy 350 kJ (85 Cal) | gi 32 ▼ low

HEARTY TOMATO & OLIVE PASTA SOUP

2 teaspoons olive oil
2 cloves garlic, crushed
1 medium onion, chopped
100 g (3 1/3 oz) shaved 97% fat-free ham
1 medium red capsicum (bell pepper), seeded and chopped
1 kg (2 lb) ripe tomatoes, chopped
4 cups (1 litre/32 fl oz) reduced-salt vegetable stock
1 tablespoon balsamic vinegar
400 g (13 oz) can chickpeas, rinsed and drained
155 g (5 oz) fettuccine, broken into small pieces
1/3 cup (50 g/1 2/3 oz) kalamata olives in brine, drained and roughly chopped
2 tablespoons finely shredded fresh basil

1 Heat the oil in a large pan, add the garlic and onion and cook over medium heat for 5 minutes or until the onion is golden.
2 Add the ham and chopped capsicum and cook for 5 minutes or until the ham is browned.
3 Add the tomatoes, stock and vinegar. Bring to the boil, reduce the heat and simmer for 20 minutes or until the tomatoes are pulpy.
4 Add the chickpeas and fettuccine. Simmer, stirring occasionally, for 7–10 minutes or until the pasta is cooked. Stir in the olives and basil just before serving. Serves 6
per serve | fat 5 g | protein 13.5 g | carbohydrate 31.5 g | fibre 5 g | cholesterol 14 mg | energy 955 kJ (230 Cal) | gi 35 ▼ low

hearty tomato & olive pasta soup

BAKED SPRING ROLLS

50 g (1 2/3 oz) mung bean (glass) noodles
300 g (10 oz) skinless chicken breasts, finely chopped
1 medium carrot, grated
1 medium zucchini (courgette), grated
1 cup (90 g/3 oz) bean sprouts
2 tablespoons fresh coriander (cilantro), roughly chopped
3 spring onions (scallions), sliced
1 large red chilli, seeded and thinly sliced
1 tablespoon sweet chilli sauce
1 tablespoon oyster sauce
2 teaspoons lime juice
24 rice paper rounds
canola oil spray

1 Preheat oven to 220°C (425°F/Gas 7). Line a baking tray with baking paper.
2 Put the noodles into a bowl, cover with boiling water and set aside for 10 minutes or until soft. Drain well. Cut the noodles into short lengths using kitchen scissors.
3 Put the noodles, chicken, carrot, zucchini, bean sprouts, coriander, spring onions, chilli, sweet chilli sauce, oyster sauce and lime juice into a bowl. Mix well using your hands.
4 Soak the rice paper rounds, one at a time, in lukewarm water until soft. Place a rice paper round on a clean work surface, top with 1 heaped tablespoon of the chicken mixture and roll up, folding in the sides to form a spring roll. Lightly brush the edges with water and press to seal. Repeat with the remaining rice paper rounds and chicken mixture.
5 Put the spring rolls seam-side down on the baking tray and spray lightly with the canola oil spray. Bake for 25 minutes or until the rolls are crisp and golden. Serve with your choice of dipping sauce. Makes 24

per roll | fat 1.5 g | protein 3.5 g | carbohydrate 6.5 g | fibre 0.5 g | cholesterol 14.5 mg | energy 215 kJ (50 Cal) | gi 52 ▼ low

baked spring rolls

CREAMY CARROT & GINGER SOUP

200 g (6½ oz) dried lima beans
30 g (1 oz) reduced-fat polyunsaturated margarine
750 g (1½ lb) carrots, unpeeled and chopped
1 medium leek, sliced
3 medium celery sticks, chopped
1 clove garlic, grated
10 cm (4 in) piece fresh ginger, grated
4 cups (1 litre/32 fl oz) reduced-salt vegetable stock
1 tablespoon honey
1 bay leaf
½ cup (50 g/1⅔ oz) skim milk powder
½ cup (125 g/4 oz) low-fat plain yoghurt
2 tablespoons chopped fresh flat-leaf parsley

1 Rinse the lima beans under cold water. Simmer the beans in a large pan of water for 40 minutes or until soft. Drain and remove any loose skins.
2 Melt the margarine in a large pan and add the carrots, leek, celery, garlic and ginger. Cover and cook, stirring occasionally, for 20 minutes or until the carrots are soft.
3 Add the cooked lima beans, stock, honey, bay leaf and skim milk powder. Simmer for 15 minutes or until the carrots are soft enough to puree. Cool slightly, then discard the bay leaf.
4 Puree the soup in batches until smooth. Return the soup to the cleaned pan, add the yoghurt and reheat gently. Do not boil or the yoghurt will split. Serve the soup in bowls topped with the parsley.
Serves 6

per serve | fat 4 g | protein 15 g | carbohydrate 31 g | fibre 10.5 g | cholesterol 4 mg | energy 930 kJ (220 Cal) | gi 33 ▼ low

creamy carrot & ginger soup

creamy vegetable & barley soup

CREAMY VEGETABLE & BARLEY SOUP

1 Put the barley into a large pan, cover with water and cook over medium heat for 40 minutes or until the barley is soft. Add extra water during cooking if the barley is drying out. Drain well.
2 Heat the canola oil in a large pan, add the leek and cook over medium heat for 5 minutes or until the leek is soft.
3 Add the carrots and celery and cook, covered, for 5 minutes or until the vegetables start to soften.
4 Add the parsnip, zucchini, pumpkin and stock and bring to the boil. Reduce the heat and simmer for 30 minutes or until the vegetables are soft.
5 Combine the skim milk powder with a little of the hot stock to form a thin paste. Stir the paste into the soup.
6 Add the peas, corn, parsley and barley and simmer for 5 minutes or until the vegetables are cooked.
Serves 6
per serve | fat 4.5 g | protein 17.5 g | carbohydrate 48.5 g | fibre 10.5 g | cholesterol 5.5 mg | energy 1280 kJ (305 Cal) | gi 38 ▼ low

1 cup (195 g/6½ oz) pearl barley
2 teaspoons canola oil
1 medium leek, sliced
2 large carrots, chopped
2 celery sticks, chopped
1 medium parsnip, chopped
2 medium zucchini (courgette), thickly sliced
300 g (10 oz) pumpkin, chopped
6 cups (1.5 litres/48 fl oz) reduced-salt vegetable stock
1 cup (100 g/3⅓ oz) skim milk powder
1 cup (150 g/5 oz) fresh or frozen peas
1 cup (200 g/6½ oz) fresh or frozen corn kernels
2 tablespoons chopped fresh flat-leaf parsley

LOW-FAT CHICKEN LAKSA

100 g (3⅓ oz) dried rice vermicelli
2 teaspoons laksa paste
2 tablespoons coconut milk powder
2 cups (500 ml/16 fl oz) reduced-salt chicken stock
400 g (13 oz) skinless chicken breasts, thinly sliced
1 teaspoon lime juice
1 teaspoon brown sugar
1 bunch (155 g/5 oz) broccolini, roughly chopped
200 g (6½ oz) snowpeas
fresh coriander (cilantro) leaves, to serve

1 Put the vermicelli into a bowl, cover with boiling water and allow to stand for 10 minutes or until the noodles are soft. Rinse and drain well.
2 Heat the laksa paste in a wok over medium heat for 3 minutes or until fragrant.
3 Whisk together the coconut milk powder and stock and stir into the laksa paste. Add the chicken, cover and simmer for 15 minutes. Season with the lime juice and brown sugar.
4 Remove the chicken and cool slightly before slicing. Add the broccolini and snowpeas to the wok and simmer until the vegetables are just tender.
5 Divide the noodles among 4 shallow bowls and mound in the center. Arrange the broccolini, snowpeas and chicken around the outside. Ladle the stock over the noodles and serve garnished with coriander leaves. Serves 4

per serve | fat 11 g | protein 29 g | carbohydrate 22.5 g | fibre 5 g | cholesterol 66 mg | energy 1285 kJ (305 Cal) | gi 45 ▼ low

low-fat chicken laksa

LUNCH

cajun fish wraps

CAJUN FISH WRAPS

350 g (12 oz) skinless, boneless white fish fillets
1½ teaspoons Cajun seasoning
1 teaspoon lemon zest
1 tablespoon lemon juice
canola oil spray
4 medium (280 g/9 oz) wholemeal pita bread
2 cups (115 g/3⅔ oz) finely shredded lettuce
2 medium vine-ripened tomatoes, roughly chopped
12 slices pickled cucumber
¼ cup (60 g/2 oz) reduced-fat Greek-style plain yoghurt

1 Pat the fish dry using absorbent paper. Cut the fish into 2 cm (¾ in) thick strips and put it into a bowl. Sprinkle with the Cajun seasoning, lemon zest and lemon juice and gently toss to combine.

2 Spread the fish strips on a non-stick baking tray, spray lightly with canola oil spray and cook under a grill preheated to high, turning occasionally, for 3-5 minutes or until the fish is tender. Drain on absorbent paper.

3 Place the opened pita bread on a flat surface. Divide the lettuce, tomatoes, pickled cucumber, fish and yoghurt among the bread. Serves 4

per serve | fat 3 g | protein 26 g | carbohydrate 41.5 g | fibre 6.5 g | cholesterol 52.5 mg | energy 1265 kJ (300 Cal) | gi 51 ▼ low

JAPANESE SOBA NOODLE SALAD

200 g (6½ oz) dried soba noodles
2 tablespoons sesame seeds
1 medium carrot, unpeeled and julienned
1 medium Lebanese cucumber, unpeeled and julienned
3 spring onions (scallions), sliced
¼ cup (60 ml/2 fl oz) reduced-salt soy sauce
1 teaspoon sugar
¼ cup (60 ml/2 fl oz) dashi stock
1 sheet (5 g/¼ oz) nori seaweed, finely shredded

1 Cook the soba noodles in a large pan of cold water until they come to the boil, add another cup of water and stir until they return to the boil. Cook for 5 minutes or until tender. Rinse under cold running water. Place the noodles into a large bowl, add a few ice cubes, cover with cold water and leave to stand.

2 Toast the sesame seeds in a fry pan, then lightly crush them in a mortar and pestle or spice grinder.

3 Drain the noodles, put into a bowl with the sesame seeds, carrot, cucumber and spring onions and toss to combine.

4 Whisk together the soy sauce, sugar and stock.

5 Top the noodles with the nori and accompany with wasabi and pickled ginger. Serve the dressing to the side. Serves 6

per serve | fat 2.5 g | protein 6.5 g | carbohydrate 27 g | fibre 3 g | cholesterol 0 mg | energy 620 kJ (150 Cal) | gi 45 ▼ low

japanese soba noodle salad

lentil & sweet potato patties

LENTIL & SWEET POTATO PATTIES

1 Cook the lentils in a large pan of boiling water for 30 minutes or until tender. Drain well.
2 Cook the rice and sweet potato in separate pans of boiling water until tender. Drain well.
3 Preheat oven to 200°C (400°F/Gas 6).
4 Combine the lentils, rice, sweet potato, spring onions, lemon juice, lemon zest, curry paste and coriander.
5 Shape the mixture into 12 patties. Roll each patty in the breadcrumbs and place onto a non-stick baking tray. Spray lightly with canola oil spray and bake for 30 minutes or until crisp and golden. Serve with a green salad. Makes 12

2/3 cup (125 g/4 oz) brown lentils
1/3 cup (70 g/2 1/4 oz) basmati rice
500 g (1 lb) orange sweet potato, chopped
4 spring onions (scallions), sliced
juice and zest of 1 lemon
1 tablespoon Madras curry paste
2 tablespoons chopped fresh coriander (cilantro)
2 cups (140 g/4 1/2 oz) fresh wholegrain breadcrumbs
canola oil spray

per patty | fat 1.5 g | protein 5.5 g | carbohydrate 23 g | fibre 3 g | cholesterol 0 mg | energy 530 kJ (125 Cal) | gi 55 ▼ low

TERIYAKI CHICKEN BURGERS

1 Toast the sesame seeds in a fry pan.
2 Put the chicken, ginger, soybeans, spring onions, teriyaki marinade, egg white, breadcrumbs and sesame seeds into a bowl and mix to combine. Shape the mixture into 6 flat patties.
3 Lightly spray a non-stick fry pan with canola oil spray, add the patties and cook over medium heat for 10-15 minutes or until cooked through.
4 Toast the rolls and top with the snowpea shoots, cucumber, a chicken patty, mayonnaise and wasabi. Serves 6

2 tablespoons sesame seeds
500 g (1 lb) lean chicken mince
1 tablespoon grated fresh ginger
300 g (10 oz) can soybeans, rinsed and drained
3 spring onions (scallions), sliced
1 tablespoon teriyaki marinade
1 egg white, lightly beaten
1 cup (70 g/2 1/4 oz) fresh wholegrain breadcrumbs
canola oil spray
6 (400 g/13 oz) wholegrain bread rolls
100 g (3 1/3 oz) snowpea shoots
1 medium Lebanese cucumber, unpeeled and sliced
2 tablespoons low-fat mayonnaise
1/2 teaspoon wasabi

per serve | fat 15 g | protein 30 g | carbohydrate 49 g | fibre 7.5 g | cholesterol 77 mg | energy 1890 kJ (450 Cal) | gi 49 ▼ low

teriyaki chicken burgers

thai chicken noodle cakes

THAI CHICKEN NOODLE CAKES

canola oil spray
100 g (3⅓ oz) 99% fat-free instant noodles
400 g (13 oz) lean chicken mince
1 teaspoon ground coriander
1 teaspoon ground cumin
1 teaspoon green curry paste
2 tablespoons chopped fresh mint
1 teaspoon lime zest
1 tablespoon lime juice
3 egg whites, lightly beaten

1 Preheat oven to 190°C (375°F/Gas 5). Lightly spray a 12 x ⅓ cup (80 ml/2⅔ fl oz) capacity non-stick muffin pan with canola oil spray.
2 Put the noodles into a pan of boiling water and cook over high heat for 2 minutes or until soft. Drain well.
3 Put the noodles, chicken mince, coriander, cumin, curry paste, mint, lime zest, lime juice and egg whites into a bowl and mix to combine.
4 Divide the mixture evenly among the muffin holes, pressing down firmly. Bake for 20 minutes or until cooked through. Drain off any excess liquid. Serve hot or cold with salad. Makes 12

per noodle cake | fat 3 g | protein 7.5 g | carbohydrate 1.25 g | fibre 0.2 g | cholesterol 30 mg | energy 260 kJ (60 Cal) | gi 46 ▼ low

SPEEDY STEAK SANDWICH

olive oil spray
4 (600 g/1 lb 3 oz) lean minute beef steaks
2 medium onions, thinly sliced
1 tablespoon balsamic vinegar
8 slices (400 g/13 oz) wholegrain bread
50 g (1⅔ oz) roughly shredded cos lettuce
2 medium tomatoes, sliced
1 large carrot, grated
1 large raw beetroot, unpeeled and grated
2 tablespoons chunky tomato salsa
2 tablespoons low-fat plain yoghurt

1 Lightly spray a chargrill pan with olive oil spray, add the steaks and cook over medium-high heat for 1 minute each side or until cooked to your liking. Remove from the pan.
2 Add the onions and balsamic vinegar and cook over medium heat for 5 minutes or until the onions are soft and sticky.
3 Toast the bread until crisp and brown. Place 4 slices on a board and top with some lettuce, tomatoes, carrot, beetroot, steak, onion, salsa and yoghurt. Finish with another slice of bread and serve immediately. Serves 4

per serve | fat 11 g | protein 45 g | carbohydrate 57.5 g | fibre 10.5 g | cholesterol 89 mg | energy 2135 kJ (510 Cal) | gi 47 ▼ low

speedy steak sandwich

pasta niçoise with lemon pepper dressing

PASTA NICOISE WITH LEMON PEPPER DRESSING

1 Cook the ravioli in a large pan of rapidly boiling water for 5 minutes, then add the beans and cook for another 5 minutes or until the beans are tender and the pasta is al dente (cooked, but still with a bite to it). Remove and drain well.
2 Put the pasta, beans, tomatoes, olives, artichoke hearts, cucumber, capsicum, tuna and basil into a bowl. Mix gently to combine.
3 Whisk together the lemon juice, garlic, olive oil and pepper, drizzle over the salad and toss gently to combine.
4 Grate the eggs over the top of the salad and serve immediately. Serves 6
per serve | fat 7.5 g | protein 21 g | carbohydrate 21 g | fibre 4.5 g | cholesterol 108.5 mg | energy 995 kJ (240 Cal) | gi 42 ▼ low

375 g (12 oz) ricotta and spinach filled pasta (agnolotti, ravioli)
200 g (6½ oz) trimmed green beans
200 g (6½ oz) cherry tomatoes, cut into wedges
50 g (1⅔ oz) kalamata olives
100 g (3⅓ oz) artichoke hearts in brine, drained
1 medium Lebanese cucumber, unpeeled and sliced
1 medium green capsicum (bell pepper), sliced
400 g (13 oz) can chunk-style tuna in spring water, drained
2 tablespoons fresh basil leaves
2 tablespoons lemon juice
1 clove garlic, crushed
2 teaspoons extra virgin olive oil
1 teaspoon cracked black pepper
2 hard-boiled eggs

ANGEL HAIR PASTA WITH HAM & LENTILS

1 Heat the oil in a large pan, add the onion, garlic and ham and cook over medium heat for 5 minutes or until the onion is golden and the ham is brown.
2 Add the lentils, tomatoes and water and bring to the boil. Reduce the heat and simmer for 25 minutes or until the lentils are soft.
3 Add the chilli and pasta and cook for 3 minutes, stirring occasionally until the pasta is al dente (cooked, but still with a bite to it). Stir through the parsley and serve. Serves 6
per serve | fat 3.5 g | protein 16 g | carbohydrate 39.5 g | fibre 7.5 g | cholesterol 8.5 mg | energy 1045 kJ (250 Cal) | gi 38 ▼ low

2 teaspoons olive oil
1 medium onion, thinly sliced
2 cloves garlic, grated
100 g (3⅓ oz) sliced 97% fat-free ham
200 g (6½ oz) brown lentils
400 g (13 oz) can chopped tomatoes
5 cups (1.25 litres/40 fl oz) water
1 teaspoon chilli flakes
200 g (6½ oz) angel hair pasta, broken into 4 cm (1½ in) pieces
2 tablespoons chopped fresh flat-leaf parsley

angel hair pasta with ham & lentils

spaghetti with chunky tuna puttanesca

SPAGHETTI WITH CHUNKY TUNA PUTTANESCA

500 g (1 lb) spaghetti
2 teaspoons olive oil
2 (500 g/1 lb) tuna steaks, cut into 3 cm (1¼ in) thick strips
200 g (6½ oz) cherry tomatoes, halved
1 large ripe tomato, chopped
50 g (1⅔ oz) kalamata olives in brine, drained and halved
2 tablespoons capers
2 anchovies in brine, drained and sliced
2 tablespoons fresh basil leaves, finely shredded
1 teaspoon lemon zest

1 Cook the spaghetti in a large pan of rapidly boiling water until al dente (cooked, but still with a bite to it). Drain well and keep warm.
2 Heat the oil in a non-stick fry pan, add the tuna steaks and cook over medium heat for 3 minutes each side. Set aside to cool slightly, then cut into thick slices.
3 Put the tuna, tomato, olives, capers, anchovies, basil and lemon zest into a large bowl. Add the spaghetti and gently toss to combine. Serves 6
per serve | fat 7.5 g | protein 31 g | carbohydrate 60.5 g | fibre 4 g | cholesterol 31 mg | energy 1835 kJ (440 Cal) | gi 41 ▼ low*

* The GI will depend on the type of spaghetti used. Longer boiling times can increase the GI value.

SPINACH & FETTA TRIANGLES

½ cup (90 g/3 oz) bulgur wheat
1 cup (250 ml/8 fl oz) water
600 g (1 lb 3 oz) trimmed English spinach
6 spring onions (scallions), sliced
2 tablespoons capers, roughly chopped
100 g (3⅓ oz) reduced-fat fetta cheese, crumbled
⅓ cup (40 g/1⅓ oz) grated reduced-fat cheddar cheese
2 eggs, lightly beaten
2 tablespoons chopped fresh mint
2 tablespoons chopped fresh dill
8 sheets filo pastry
olive oil spray

1 Preheat oven to 220°C (425°F/Gas 7).
2 Put the bulgur wheat and water into a bowl and leave for 15 minutes or until the water is absorbed.
3 Wash the spinach. Cook, covered, in a pan over medium heat for 3-5 minutes or until wilted. Cool slightly, then drain and roughly chop the leaves.
4 Combine the spinach, bulgur wheat, spring onions, capers, cheeses, eggs and herbs in a bowl.
5 Lightly spray one sheet of filo with olive oil spray. Top with another sheet of filo and cut in half lengthwise. Place 2 tablespoons of the spinach mixture on the end of each strip. Fold up diagonally to enclose the filling. Repeat with the remaining pastry and filling. Bake on a non-stick baking tray for 20 minutes or until crisp and golden. Makes 8
per triangle | fat 5.5 g | protein 11 g | carbohydrate 16 g | fibre 4.5 g | cholesterol 57.5 mg | energy 655 kJ (155 Cal) | gi 50 ▼ low

spinach & fetta triangles

DINNER

chicken, apricot & sweet potato pies

CHICKEN, APRICOT & SWEET POTATO PIES

2 teaspoons canola oil
1 medium leek, sliced
350 g (12 oz) chicken thighs, sliced
300 g (10 oz) orange sweet potato, cut into 3 cm (1 1/4 in) cubes
1/2 cup (125 ml/4 fl oz) reduced-salt chicken stock
100 g (3 1/3 oz) dried apricot halves
1-2 tablespoons arrowroot
2 tablespoons chopped fresh basil
4 sheets filo pastry
canola oil spray

1 Preheat oven to 200°C (400°F/Gas 6).
2 Heat the oil in a non-stick fry pan, add the leek and cook over medium heat for 5 minutes or until golden. Cook the chicken for 5 minutes or until browned.
3 Add the sweet potato, stock and apricots. Bring to the boil, reduce the heat and simmer for 15 minutes or until the chicken is tender and the sauce is thick.
4 Combine the arrowroot with a little of the hot stock and stir into the chicken mixture until the sauce boils and thickens. Remove from the heat. Stir in the basil.
5 Cut the pastry sheets in half and fold into quarters. Line 4 x 10 cm (4 in) pie dishes with pastry and lightly spray with canola oil spray. Continue layering and spraying with the remaining pastry. Spoon the hot pie mixture into the pastry, fold over the pastry and lightly spray with canola oil spray. Bake for 10-15 minutes or until crisp and golden. Serves 4

per serve | fat 9.5 g | protein 21 g | carbohydrate 33 g | fibre 4.5 g | cholesterol 76 mg | energy 1270 kJ (305 Cal) | gi 44 ▼ low

ROASTED FILLED CAPSICUMS

2 medium red and 2 medium yellow capsicums (bell peppers)
100 g (3 1/3 oz) cherry tomatoes
50 g (1 2/3 oz) kalamata olives
400 g (13 oz) can chickpeas, drained
1 medium onion, sliced
1 medium zucchini (courgette), thickly sliced
100 g (3 1/3 oz) sun-dried tomatoes
1 tablespoon fresh oregano leaves
2 cloves garlic, sliced
100 g (3 1/3 oz) reduced-fat fetta cheese
cracked black pepper

1 Preheat oven to 200°C (400°F/Gas 6).
2 Cut the capsicums in half and remove the seeds.
3 Arrange the tomatoes, olives, chickpeas, onion, zucchini, sun-dried tomatoes, oregano, garlic and fetta in the capsicum shells. Season with cracked black pepper.
4 Place on a non-stick baking tray and bake for 30 minutes or until the capsicums are soft and the filling is hot. Serves 4

per serve | fat 6.5 g | protein 15.5 g | carbohydrate 25.5 g | fibre 8.0 g | cholesterol 15 mg | energy 940 kJ (225 Cal) | gi 27 ▼ low

roasted filled capsicums

thai prawn & noodle stir fry

THAI PRAWN & NOODLE STIR FRY

1 Heat the oil in a wok until smoking, add the ginger, garlic, spring onions, chilli and prawns and stir fry over medium heat until the prawns turn pink. Remove from the wok.
2 Add the snake beans, Chinese broccoli and a generous splash of water and stir fry until the vegetables are bright green.
3 Add the noodles, soy sauce, oyster sauce, sugar and stock and stir fry until the noodles soften.
4 Return the prawn mixture to the wok and stir fry until heated through. Serve sprinkled with cracked black pepper and garnished with bean sprouts. Serves 4
per serve | fat 4 g | protein 34 g | carbohydrate 56 g | fibre 4 g | cholesterol 186 mg | energy 1680 kJ (500 Cal) | gi 38 ▼ low

2 teaspoons canola oil
1 tablespoon grated fresh ginger
1 clove garlic, crushed
4 spring onions (scallions), sliced
1 large red chilli, seeded and sliced
500 g (1 lb) peeled and deveined green prawns
250 g (8 oz) snake beans, chopped
250 g (8 oz) Chinese broccoli, cut into 5 cm (2 in) lengths
500 g (1 lb) fresh rice noodles
2 tablespoons reduced-salt soy sauce
1 tablespoon oyster sauce
1 teaspoon caster sugar
¼ cup (60 ml/2 fl oz) reduced-salt chicken stock
cracked black pepper
50 g (1²⁄₃ oz) bean sprouts

BEEF WITH CORN & CAPSICUM RELISH

1 Cook the corn and capsicums in a preheated chargrill pan, turning, for 10 minutes or until the corn is tender and the capsicums blisters and blackens. Transfer the capsicums to a plastic bag to cool. Peel away the skin and cut the flesh into strips. Cut the corn into pieces.
2 Heat the oil on a barbecue flat plate. Cook the onion for 10 minutes or until soft and browned. Cook the tomatoes until the skins start to split. Combine the onion, tomatoes, corn, capsicum, vinegar and mustard.
3 Cook the steaks on a barbecue chargrill until done to your liking. Serve with the beans and relish. Serves 4
per serve | fat 15 g | protein 45.5 g | carbohydrate 24 g | fibre 6.5 g | cholesterol 113 mg | energy 1745 kJ (415 Cal) | gi 37 ▼ low

2 medium cobs sweet corn
2 medium red capsicums (bell peppers)
2 teaspoons olive oil
1 medium red (Spanish) onion, thinly sliced
200 g (6½ oz) cherry tomatoes
1 tablespoon red wine vinegar
2 teaspoons wholegrain honey mustard
4 (780 g/1½ lb) lean beef sirloin steaks, trimmed
300 g (10 oz) green beans, trimmed and steamed

beef with corn & capsicum relish

saffron salmon with mediterranean salad

SAFFRON SALMON WITH MEDITERRANEAN SALAD

pinch of saffron threads
4 (630 g/1¼ lb) salmon fillets
1 lemon, thinly sliced
juice of 1 lemon
1 tablespoon fresh rosemary
olive oil spray
cracked black pepper
400 g (13 oz) can butter beans, rinsed and drained
1 red (Spanish) onion, thinly sliced
100 g (3⅓ oz) cherry tomatoes, halved
40 g (1⅓ oz) baby rocket (arugula)
100 g (3⅓ oz) reduced-fat fetta cheese, crumbled
2 tablespoons balsamic vinegar

1 Preheat oven to 200°C (400°F/Gas 6).
2 Put the saffron into a bowl, cover with boiling water and leave to soak for 10 minutes.
3 Put the salmon fillets onto a non-stick baking tray, top with the soaked saffron and liquid, lemon slices, lemon juice and rosemary. Spray with olive oil spray and season with cracked black pepper. Bake for 15 minutes or until the salmon is tender but still slightly pink inside.
4 Put the butter beans, onion, tomatoes, rocket and fetta into a bowl and gently toss to combine. Divide among 4 plates and drizzle with the vinegar. Serve with the salmon and any juices. Serves 4
per serve | fat 15.5 g | protein 41 g | carbohydrate 8.5 g | fibre 3.5 g | cholesterol 97 mg | energy 1425 kJ (340 Cal) | gi 28 ▼ low

SALSA VERDE LAMB RACK WITH GARLIC BEANS

4 lamb racks with 3 cutlets (430 g/15 oz), trimmed
cracked black pepper
1 head garlic
800 g (1 lb 10 oz) can butter beans, rinsed and drained
1 cup (250 ml/8 fl oz) reduced-salt chicken stock
1 cup (30 g/1 oz) roughly chopped fresh flat-leaf parsley
2 gherkins, chopped
1 tablespoon anchovies in brine, drained and chopped
2 tablespoons capers, chopped
3 cloves garlic, crushed
2 tablespoons red wine vinegar
1 tablespoon extra virgin olive oil

1 Preheat oven to 220°C (425°F/Gas 7).
2 Season the lamb racks with cracked black pepper. Put the lamb and garlic into a baking dish and bake for 15-20 minutes or until cooked to your liking. Leave for 5 minutes before slicing into cutlets.
3 Meanwhile, put the beans and stock into a pan and bring to the boil. Reduce the heat and simmer, covered, for 30 minutes or until soft. Cool slightly, then transfer to a food processor. Add the peeled roasted garlic and process until roughly mashed.
4 Put the parsley, gherkins, anchovies, capers, garlic, vinegar and oil into a bowl and mix to combine.
5 Serve the lamb on a bed of garlic beans with the salsa verde on the side. Serves 4
per serve | fat 12.5 g | protein 28.5 g | carbohydrate 8 g | fibre 5.5 g | cholesterol 73 mg | energy 1085 kJ (260 Cal) | gi 16 ▼ low

salsa verde lamb rack with garlic beans

CHICKPEA VEGETABLE CURRY WITH LEMON RICE

2 teaspoons canola oil
1 teaspoon brown mustard seeds
1 medium onion, chopped
2 tablespoons Madras curry paste
1 medium carrot, cut into 3 cm (1¼ in) pieces
500 g (1 lb) orange sweet potato, cut into 3 cm (1¼ in) pieces
2 medium zucchini (courgette), cut into 3 cm (1¼ in) pieces
400 g (13 oz) can peeled tomatoes
400 g (13 oz) can chickpeas, rinsed and drained
1½ cups (375 ml/12 fl oz) water
200 g (6½ oz) green beans, halved
¼ cup (60 g/2 oz) low-fat plain yoghurt
1 tablespoon chopped fresh coriander (cilantro)
2 cups (410 g/13½ oz) basmati rice
15 fresh curry leaves
1 tablespoon lemon juice
2 teaspoons lemon zest
4 cups (1 litre/32 fl oz) water, extra

1 Heat the oil in a large pan, add the mustard seeds and onion and cook over medium heat for 5 minutes or until the onion is golden. Add the curry paste and cook for 2 minutes or until fragrant.
2 Add the carrot, sweet potato and zucchini and cook for 3 minutes or until the vegetables start to soften. Add the tomatoes, chickpeas and water. Bring to the boil, reduce the heat and simmer for 15 minutes.
3 Add the beans and cook for 5 minutes or until the vegetables are soft. Remove from the heat and stir through the yoghurt and coriander.
4 Meanwhile, put the rice, curry leaves, lemon juice, lemon zest and extra water into a pan, bring to the boil and cook over high heat until tunnels appear in the rice. Reduce the heat to low, cover and cook for 15 minutes or until the rice is soft.
5 Serve the curry with pots of the rice to the side.
Serves 6
per serve | fat 5.5 g | protein 12 g | carbohydrate 78 g | fibre 7.5 g | cholesterol 0.5 mg | energy 1730 kJ (415 Cal) | gi 52 ▼ low

chickpea vegetable curry with lemon rice

CHICKEN WITH PESTO BARLEY

4 (840 g/1 lb 11 oz) skinless chicken breasts
250 g (8 oz) baby English spinach
125 g (4 oz) reduced-fat creamed cottage cheese
¼ cup (40 g/1⅓ oz) semi-dried tomatoes, roughly chopped
1 teaspoon lemon zest
olive oil spray
250 g (8 oz) barley
2 cups (60 g/2 oz) fresh basil leaves
2 cloves garlic
2 tablespoons finely grated parmesan cheese
2 teaspoons extra virgin olive oil

1 Preheat oven to 200°C (400°F/Gas 6).
2 Cut a pocket through the middle of each chicken breast, taking care not to cut all the way through.
3 Wash the spinach. Cook, covered, in a pan over medium heat for 3-5 minutes or until wilted. Cool slightly, then drain and roughly chop the leaves.
4 Put the spinach, cottage cheese, semi-dried tomatoes and lemon zest into a bowl and mix to combine. Stuff each chicken pocket with the spinach mixture and secure with toothpicks.
5 Lightly spray a non-stick fry pan with olive oil spray and heat over medium heat. Add the chicken and brown on both sides. Transfer to a baking tray, cover with foil and bake for 15 minutes or until tender.
6 Put the barley into a large pan, cover with water and cook over medium heat for 40 minutes or until the barley is soft. Add extra water during cooking if the barley is drying out. Drain well.
7 Put the basil, garlic and parmesan into a food processor and process to form a smooth paste. Gradually add the oil with the motor running until combined. Add to the barley and mix to combine.
8 Serve the sliced chicken breasts with the pesto barley to the side. Serves 4

per serve | fat 19 g | protein 59.5 g | carbohydrate 43 g | fibre 11 g | cholesterol 149.5 mg | energy 2550 kJ (605 Cal) | gi 25 ▼ low*

* The GI will depend on the type of barley used. The coarser and less processed the barley, the lower the GI value.

chicken with pesto barley

sweet potato shepherds' pie

SWEET POTATO SHEPHERDS' PIE

1 Preheat oven to 200°C (400°F/Gas 6).
2 Heat the oil in a non-stick pan, add the onion and cook over medium heat for 5 minutes or until the onion is golden. Add the carrots and celery and cook for 3 minutes or until the vegetables start to soften.
3 Add the mince and cook for 5 minutes or until browned. Add the corn, thyme, tomato paste, flour and Worcestershire sauce and stir until smooth. Add the water and stir until the sauce boils and thickens slightly. Reduce the heat and simmer for 15 minutes.
4 Cook the sweet potato in a large pan of boiling water for 15 minutes or until very soft. Drain well and mash.
5 Heat the margarine in a non-stick fry pan, add the leek and cook over medium heat for 5 minutes or until soft.
6 Spoon the meat mixture into a 30 cm x 20 cm (12 in x 8 in) ovenproof dish or 6 x 1 cup (250 ml/ 8 fl oz) capacity individual pie dishes. Spread the sweet potato over the meat, top with the leek and sprinkle with the cheese. Bake for 20 minutes or until the cheese is golden and the pie is heated through. Serves 6

per serve | **fat 12.5 g** | **protein 32 g** | **carbohydrate 32.5 g** | **fibre 6 g** | **cholesterol 88 mg** | **energy 1545 kJ (370 Cal)** | **gi 42** ▼ **low**

2 teaspoons olive oil
1 medium onion, chopped
2 medium carrots, chopped
2 medium celery sticks, chopped
750 g (1½ lb) lean lamb mince
1 cup (200 g/6½ oz) fresh or frozen corn kernels
2 teaspoons chopped fresh thyme
1 tablespoon tomato paste
1 tablespoon plain flour
1 tablespoon Worcestershire sauce
1 cup (250 ml/8 fl oz) water
1 kg (2 lb) orange sweet potato, chopped
10 g (1/3 oz) reduced-fat polyunsaturated margarine
1 medium leek, sliced
2 tablespoons grated reduced-fat cheddar cheese

chicken with creamy mushrooms

CHICKEN WITH CREAMY MUSHROOMS

1 Heat a non-stick fry pan, add the chicken and cook over medium-high heat for 5 minutes or until browned. Reduce the heat, add the water, cover and cook for 10 minutes or until tender.
2 Cook the lentils in a pan of boiling water for 20 minutes or until tender. Drain well.
3 Heat the oil in a fry pan, add the spring onions and garlic and cook over medium heat for 3 minutes or until golden. Add the mushrooms and cook until soft and brown. Add the wine and cook over high heat until all the liquid has evaporated.
4 Add the stock and evaporated milk and bring to the boil, reduce the heat, add the chicken and simmer for 15 minutes or until the chicken is tender. Remove the chicken and keep warm.
5 Combine the cornflour with the extra water to form a smooth paste. Stir the paste into the stock mixture and cook, stirring, until the sauce boils and thickens.
6 Wash the spinach. Cook, covered, in a pan over medium heat for 3-5 minutes or until wilted.
7 Spoon the lentils onto 4 plates and top with mounds of the spinach and the chicken. Pour the sauce over the top. Serves 4

per serve | fat 16 g | protein 64.5 g | carbohydrate 27 g | fibre 10.5 g | cholesterol 141.5 mg | energy 2210 kJ (530 Cal) | gi 26 ▼ low

4 (840 g/1 lb 11 oz) skinless chicken breasts
1/4 cup (60 ml/2 fl oz) water
200 g (6 1/2 oz) lentils du puy
2 teaspoons olive oil
3 spring onions (scallions), sliced
2 cloves garlic, crushed
200 g (6 1/2 oz) Swiss brown mushrooms, sliced
1/2 cup (125 ml/4 fl oz) white wine
1 cup (250 ml/8 fl oz) reduced-salt chicken stock
1/2 cup (125 ml/4 fl oz) reduced-fat evaporated milk
1 tablespoon cornflour
2 tablespoons water, extra
300 g (10 oz) trimmed English spinach

SWEET THINGS

mango lime jellies

MANGO LIME JELLIES

3 cups (750 ml/24 fl oz) unsweetened apple and mango juice
6 teaspoons gelatin
6 kaffir lime leaves, finely shredded

1 Put ½ cup (125 ml/4 fl oz) of the juice into a pan, add the gelatin and stir over low heat until the gelatin dissolves.
2 Add the remaining juice and lime leaves and bring to the boil, reduce the heat and simmer for 5 minutes. Remove from the heat, strain and discard the leaves.
3 Wet 6 x ½ cup (125 ml/4 fl oz) capacity jelly moulds, fill with the jelly mixture and refrigerate for 4 hours or until set. Serves 6

per serve | fat 0.01 g | protein 2.5 g | carbohydrate 13.5 g | fibre 0 g | cholesterol 0 mg | energy 270 kJ (65 Cal) | gi 44 ▼ low

LITTLE UPSIDE-DOWN APPLE CAKES

425 g (14 oz) can pie apple
60 g (2 oz) reduced-fat polyunsaturated margarine
½ cup (125 g/4 oz) caster sugar or ½ cup (13 g/½ oz) low-calorie sweetener suitable for cooking
1 egg, lightly beaten
¾ cup (105 g/3½ oz) stone-ground wholemeal self-raising flour
3 tablespoons plain flour
½ cup (125 ml/4 fl oz) reduced-fat milk

1 Preheat oven to 180°C (350°F/Gas 4). Line the bases of an 8 x ⅓ cup (80 ml/2⅔ fl oz) capacity non-stick muffin pan with baking paper.
2 Divide the apple among the muffin holes.
3 Beat the margarine and sugar or sweetener until light and creamy. Beat in the egg until combined.
4 Fold in the sifted flours and milk and mix until smooth. Divide the mixture evenly among the muffin holes and smooth the surface. Bake for 20 minutes or until a skewer comes out clean when inserted into the center. Cool for 5 minutes in the pan before turning out on a wire rack. Serve warm with low-fat vanilla custard or no-fat, no-added sugar vanilla yoghurt. Makes 8

per cake (sugar) | fat 5.5 g | protein 3 g | carbohydrate 34.5 g | fibre 1.5 g | cholesterol 24 mg | energy 815 kJ (195 Cal) | gi 57 ♦ med
per cake (sweetener) | fat 5.5 g | protein 3 g | carbohydrate 20.5 g | fibre 1.5 g | cholesterol 24 mg | energy 590 kJ (140 Cal) | gi 49 ▼ low

little upside-down apple cakes

plum & custard sponge cake

PLUM & CUSTARD SPONGE CAKE

1 Line a 20 cm (8 in) spring form tin with baking paper.
2 Put the plum juice and brandy into a pan, bring to the boil and cook over high heat for 10 minutes. Transfer to a shallow dish. Set aside to cool.
3 Dip half the biscuits into the syrup and arrange over the base of the tin. Top with half the plums.
4 Beat the cream cheese and ricotta until smooth and creamy, add the custard and beat until combined. Spoon a third of the mixture over the plums. Repeat layering the biscuits, plums and custard mixture, finishing with the custard. Cover and refrigerate overnight. Sprinkle with nutmeg to serve. Serves 10
per serve | fat 5.5 g | protein 7 g | carbohydrate 30.5 g | fibre 1 g | cholesterol 56.5 mg | energy 860 kJ (205 Cal) | gi 44 ▼ low

800 g (1 lb 10 oz) can plums in natural juice, drained and roughly chopped, juice reserved
¼ cup (60 ml/2 fl oz) brandy
250 g (8 oz) sponge finger biscuits
125 g (4 oz) reduced-fat cream cheese, softened
250 g (8 oz) low-fat smooth ricotta cheese
1 cup (250 ml/8 fl oz) low-fat vanilla custard
ground nutmeg

GREEN APPLE SORBET

1 Put the apple and lime juice into a food processor and process until smooth. Strain the puree through a fine sieve, reserving 1 cup (250 ml/8 fl oz) of juice.
2 Put the sugar or sweetener and water into a small pan and stir over low heat until the sugar dissolves. Remove from the heat and cool slightly.
3 Add the reserved juice and sparkling apple juice to the sugar syrup and pour into a shallow metal tray.
4 Freeze for 3-4 hours. Scoop the mixture into a food processor. With the motor running, gradually add the egg white and process until light and fluffy. Return to the freezer and freeze until firm. Serves 6
per serve (sugar) | fat 0.15 g | protein 1 g | carbohydrate 28 g | fibre 2 g | cholesterol 0 mg | energy 485 kJ (115 Cal) | gi 52 ▼ low
per serve (sweetener) | fat 0.15 g | protein 1 g | carbohydrate 18 g | fibre 2 g | cholesterol 0 mg | energy 320 kJ (75 Cal) | gi 42 ▼ low

4 Granny Smith apples (750 g/ 1½ lb), unpeeled, cored and roughly chopped
juice of 2 limes
⅓ cup (85 g/2¾ oz) caster sugar or ⅓ cup (8 g/¼ oz) low-calorie sweetener suitable for cooking
2 cups (500 ml/16 fl oz) water
1 cup (250 ml/8 fl oz) unsweetened sparkling apple juice
1 egg white

green apple sorbet

rhubarb & strawberry rice pudding

RHUBARB & STRAWBERRY RICE PUDDING

1 cup (220 g/7 oz) arborio rice
2 cups (500 ml/16 fl oz) water
3 cups (750 ml/24 fl oz) skim or no-fat milk
1 bunch trimmed rhubarb, leaves discarded (230 g/7¼ oz), cut into 3 cm (1¼ in) pieces
¼ cup (60 ml/2 fl oz) unsweetened apple juice
3 tablespoons caster sugar or low-calorie sweetener suitable for cooking
1 vanilla bean, halved lengthwise
200 g (6½ oz) strawberries, halved

1 Put the rice and water into a pan, bring to the boil without stirring and cook over medium heat for 5 minutes or until most of the water is absorbed.
2 Add the milk and bring to the boil, reduce the heat and simmer for 20 minutes, stirring occasionally until the rice is soft.
3 Put the rhubarb, apple juice, sugar or sweetener and vanilla bean into a pan and gently stir over low heat until the sugar dissolves. Cover and cook for 5 minutes, then add the strawberries and cook for another 5 minutes or just until the rhubarb is soft. Do not overcook or the rhubarb will break up. Remove the vanilla bean.
4 Serve the rice topped with the rhubarb and strawberries. Serves 6

per serve (sugar) | fat 0.5 g | protein 8 g | carbohydrate 46.5 g | fibre 2 g | cholesterol 4 mg | energy 935 kJ (225 Cal) | gi 59 ◆ med
per serve (sweetener) | fat 0.5 g | protein 8 g | carbohydrate 39 g | fibre 2 g | cholesterol 4 mg | energy 820 kJ (195 Cal) | gi 58 ◆ med

PASSIONFRUIT ICE CREAM SANDWICHES

1 cup (175 g/5⅔ oz) low-fat, low-GI vanilla ice cream, softened
195 g (6½ oz) passionfruit low-fat frozen fruit dessert
2 tablespoons passionfruit pulp
1 tablespoon finely shredded fresh mint (optional)
8 ice cream wafers

1 Put the ice cream, passionfruit dessert, passionfruit pulp and mint into a bowl and mix to combine.
2 Spread the ice cream over half the ice cream wafers and sandwich together with the remaining wafers. Freeze until firm. Makes 4

per serve | fat 3 g | protein 4 g | carbohydrate 25 g | fibre 1.5 g | cholesterol 4.5 mg | energy 610 kJ (145 Cal) | gi 47 ▼ low*

*The GI will depend on the type of ice cream used.

passionfruit ice cream sandwiches

cherryberry cobbler

CHERRYBERRY COBBLER

1 Preheat oven to 190°C (375°F/Gas 5).
2 Put the berries, cherries, 1 tablespoon of the sugar or sweetener, lime zest, lime juice and vanilla extract into a bowl and mix gently to combine. Spoon the mixture into a shallow rectangular ovenproof dish.
3 Sift the flour, baking powder, mixed spice and remaining sugar or sweetener into a bowl. Rub in the margarine until it resembles fine breadcrumbs. Stir in the buttermilk and mix to a soft smooth dough.
4 Drop large spoonfuls of the dough over the top of the berry mixture. Bake for 40 minutes or until the dumplings are golden brown. Serves 6
per serve (sugar) | fat 6.5 g | protein 7.5 g | carbohydrate 37.5 g | fibre 6.5 g | cholesterol 4 mg | energy 990 kJ (235 Cal) | gi 52 ▼ low
per serve (sweetener) | fat 6.5 g | protein 7.5 g | carbohydrate 30 g | fibre 6.5 g | cholesterol 4 mg | energy 870 kJ (210 Cal) | gi 48 ▼ low

750 g (1½ lb) mixed fresh berries (strawberries, blackberries, blueberries, raspberries)
425 g (14 oz) can pitted cherries, drained
3 tablespoons caster sugar or low-calorie sweetener suitable for cooking
1 teaspoon lime zest
2 teaspoons lime juice
1 teaspoon vanilla extract
1 cup (140 g/4½ oz) stone-ground wholemeal plain flour
2 teaspoons baking powder
½ teaspoon mixed spice
50 g (1⅔ oz) reduced-fat polyunsaturated margarine
1 cup (250 ml/8 fl oz) buttermilk

BAKED CHEESECAKE

1 Preheat oven to 180°C (350°F/Gas 4). Line the base of a 20 cm (8 in) spring form tin with baking paper and lightly spray the side with canola oil spray.
2 Put the biscuits into a food processor and process until finely crushed. Add the margarine and mix to combine. Press into the tin and refrigerate until firm.
3 Put the ricotta, cream cheese, sugar and juice into a food processor and beat until smooth and creamy.
4 Add the egg whites and pulse until combined. Pour into the tin and bake for 45 minutes or until just set. Turn off the oven and leave to cool in the oven.
5 Serve topped with fresh berries. Serves 10
per serve | fat 9 g | protein 6.5 g | carbohydrate 19.5 g | fibre 1 g | cholesterol 24 mg | energy 760 kJ (180 Cal) | gi 57 ◆ med

canola oil spray
65 g (2 oz) plain sweet biscuits
20 g (¾ oz) reduced-fat polyunsaturated margarine, melted
250 g (8 oz) low-fat smooth ricotta cheese
250 g (8 oz) reduced-fat cream cheese, softened
½ cup (125 g/4 oz) caster sugar
1 tablespoon lemon juice
2 egg whites, lightly beaten
400 g (13 oz) fresh berries, to serve

baked cheesecake

apricot & almond ice cream domes

APRICOT & ALMOND ICE CREAM DOMES

200 g (6½ oz) dried apricot halves, roughly chopped
1 cup (250 ml/8 fl oz) apricot nectar
2 cups (350 g/12 oz) low-fat, low-GI vanilla ice cream, softened
¼ cup (25 g/1 oz) flaked almonds, toasted

1 Line 8 x ½ cup (125 ml/4 fl oz) capacity friand tins or 8 mini loaf tins with plastic wrap.
2 Put half the apricots into a pan with the apricot nectar, bring to the boil and cook over medium heat for 10 minutes or until most of the liquid has been absorbed. Set aside until completely cool.
3 Spoon 2 tablespoons of apricot mixture into each tin. Fold the remaining apricots, apricot mixture and almonds through the ice cream. Spoon onto the apricot and smooth the surface. Freeze for 6 hours or until firm. Gently lift the plastic to remove. Serves 8
per serve | fat 3 g | protein 4 g | carbohydrate 24 g | fibre 2.5 g | cholesterol 4.5 mg | energy 570 kJ (135 Cal) | gi 37 ▼ low

INDIVIDUAL PRUNE & PEAR DESSERT CAKES

canola oil spray
400 g (13 oz) pears in natural juice
200 g (6½ oz) pitted prunes, roughly chopped
1 vanilla bean, halved lengthwise
12 slices fruit and spice loaf, crusts trimmed
1 egg, lightly beaten
2 egg whites, lightly beaten
1 cup (250 ml/8 fl oz) skim or no-fat milk
4 small scoops low-fat, low-GI vanilla ice cream

1 Preheat oven to 180°C (350°F/Gas 4). Lightly spray a 4 x 1 cup (250 ml/8 fl oz) capacity non-stick muffin pan with canola oil spray.
2 Drain the pears and put the juice into a pan with the prunes and vanilla bean. Bring to the boil, reduce the heat and simmer for 10 minutes or until thick.
3 Line the base of each muffin hole with a slice of bread and top with some sliced pear and some of the prune mixture. Continue layering the bread, prune and pear, finishing with a layer of bread.
4 Whisk together the egg, egg whites and milk, divide the mixture among the holes and leave for 10 minutes or until the custard has been absorbed.
5 Bake for 20 minutes or until the custard has set and the bread is puffed and golden. Remove from the tins and serve with vanilla ice cream. Serves 4
per serve | fat 5.5 g | protein 15 g | carbohydrate 82.5 g | fibre 8 g | cholesterol 50.5 mg | energy 1835 kJ (440 Cal) | gi 45 ▼ low

individual prune & pear dessert cakes

GLOSSARY

antioxidant - a substance that prevents body tissues from being damaged by oxidation caused by free radicals, which are thought to be associated with many disease processes and are formed in the body naturally or from exposure to pollution, cigarette smoking, chemicals and the sun.

carbohydrates - a group of nutrients that includes starches, sugars and fibres. All carbohydrates, except for fibres, are made up of sugar units. They are broken down into sugars during digestion. Different carbohydrates are made up of chains of sugars bound together in different ways. They are both digested and their sugar absorbed into the blood at different rates (see glycaemic index on pages 4-5).

glucose - a type of sugar that makes up the starches and some sugars found in foods. Starches are broken down into glucose during digestion, which is then absorbed into the bloodstream and becomes blood glucose (blood sugar), the main fuel for the brain and muscles.

hypoglycaemia - the term for a lower than normal blood glucose level, often called a 'hypo'. It can be due to taking too much insulin or diabetes medication; not eating enough carbohydrate or missing a meal; drinking alcohol without food; or stress or extra exercise. Symptoms include feeling cold and weak, sweating, shakiness, irritability, confusion, and dizziness, and if blood sugar continues to fall it can lead to unconsciousness and coma.

insulin - a hormone secreted by the pancreas in response to rising blood sugar, which enables body cells to take up glucose from the blood, causing the blood glucose level to drop back down to normal. It also stimulates cells to take up fats and proteins from the blood.

omega-3 essential fats - polyunsaturated fats that have to be obtained from the diet because they cannot be made in the body. They are found in walnuts, linseed, canola oil, and oily fish like tuna, salmon, trout and mackerel. Increasing the intake of omega-3 fats while reducing saturated fat intake can help improve insulin action, reduce blood pressure and promote good circulation.

sweeteners and sugar substitutes - these can be either: 1. Nutritive sweeteners, which contain calories and increase blood sugar (eg, sugar, corn syrup, fructose, glucose, honey, maltose, fruit juice concentrate); 2. Sugar alcohols, which contain fewer calories and have a lower blood sugar response (eg, sorbitol, mannitol, isomalt); or 3. Non-nutritive or low-calorie sweeteners, which are far sweeter than sugar and used in tiny amounts, so they provide almost no calories and won't increase blood sugar (eg, aspartame, acesulfame-K, Splenda®). Many 'lite' or reduced-sugar versions of sweet foods, such as soft drinks and jam, contain sugar alcohols and/or low-calorie sweeteners and can usually be consumed in moderation by people with diabetes.

INDEX

angel hair pasta with ham
 & lentils **55**
apple cakes, little upside-down **80**
apricot & almond ice cream
 domes **92**
baked cheesecake **89**
baked spring rolls **36**
banana malt smoothie **18**
beef with corn & capsicum
 relish **65**
cajun fish wraps **46**
capsicums, roasted filled **62**
carrot & ginger soup, creamy **38**
cheese & tomato french toast **13**
cheesecake, baked **89**
cherryberry cobbler **89**
chicken, apricot & sweet potato
 pies **62**
chicken burgers, teriyaki **49**
chicken with creamy mushrooms **77**
chicken laksa, low-fat **42**
chicken noodle cakes, thai **52**
chicken with pesto barley **72**
chicken soup, split pea & **28**
chickpea vegetable curry with
 lemon rice **70**
cobbler, cherryberry **89**
corn, spinach & chive omelette **23**
creamy carrot & ginger soup **38**
creamy vegetable & barley soup **41**
curry with lemon rice, chickpea
 vegetable **70**
eggs, mexican beans & **20**
fish wraps, cajun **46**
french toast, cheese & tomato **13**
green apple sorbet **83**
h.e.l.t. **10**
hearty tomato & olive pasta
 soup **34**

hummus, red capsicum **34**
ice cream domes, apricot
 & almond **92**
ice cream sandwiches,
 passionfruit **86**
individual prune & pear dessert
 cakes **92**
japanese soba noodle salad **46**
jellies, mango lime **80**
juice, sunrise **15**
lamb rack with garlic beans, salsa
 verde **68**
lentil & sweet potato patties **49**
little upside-down apple cakes **80**
low-fat chicken laksa **42**
make at home muesli **10**
mango coconut yoghurt pops **28**
mango lime jellies **80**
mango, peach & papaya summer
 salad **18**
mexican beans & eggs **20**
muesli, make at home **10**
muesli, spiced bircher **24**
omelette, corn, spinach &
 chive **23**
passionfruit ice cream
 sandwiches **86**
pasta with ham & lentils,
 angel hair **55**
pasta niçoise with lemon pepper
 dressing **55**
pie, sweet potato shepherds' **75**
pies, chicken, apricot & sweet
 potato **62**
plum & custard sponge cake **83**
prawn & noodle stir fry, thai **65**
prune & pear dessert cakes,
 individual **92**
red capsicum hummus **34**

rhubarb & strawberry rice
 pudding **86**
rice pudding, rhubarb &
 strawberry **86**
roasted filled capsicums **62**
saffron salmon with mediterranean
 salad **68**
salmon with mediterranean salad,
 saffron **68**
salsa verde lamb rack with garlic
 beans **68**
semolina with banana &
 nuts **15**
smoked salmon pumpernickel **31**
smoothie, banana malt **18**
soba noodle salad, japanese **46**
sorbet, green apple **83**
spaghetti with chunky tuna
 puttanesca **58**
speedy steak sandwich **52**
spiced bircher muesli **24**
spinach & fetta triangles **58**
split pea & chicken soup **28**
spring rolls, baked **36**
steak sandwich, speedy **52**
stir fry, thai prawn & noodle **65**
sunrise juice **15**
sweet potato shepherds' pie **75**
teriyaki chicken burgers **49**
thai chicken noodle cakes **52**
thai prawn & noodle stir fry **65**
tomato & olive pasta soup,
 hearty **34**
tuna puttanesca, spaghetti with
 chunky **58**
vegetable & barley soup,
 creamy **41**
white bean & salsa soup **31**
yoghurt pops, mango coconut **28**

96 ACKNOWLEDGEMENTS

Publisher Jody Vassallo
General manager Claire Connolly
Recipes & styling Jody Vassallo
Photographer Ben Dearnley
Home economist Penelope Grieve
Props stylist Melissa Singer
Designer Annette Fitzgerald
Editor Justine Harding
Consulting nutritionist Dr Susanna Holt

STYLING CREDITS:
Chee Soon & Fitzgerald (02) 9361 1031
Lincraft (03) 9525 8770
Made in Japan (02) 9410 3799
Mud Australia (02) 9518 0220
Orson & Blake (02) 9326 1155
Royal Doulton (02) 9499 1904
Tomkin (02) 9319 2993
Villeroy & Boch (02) 9975 3099
Wheel & Barrow (02) 9413 9530
© **Recipes** Jody Vassallo 2003
© **Photography** Ben Dearnley
© **Series design** Fortiori Publishing

PUBLISHED BY FORTIORI PUBLISHING:
PO Box 3126 Nunawading
Victoria 3131 Australia
Phone: 61 3 9872 3855
Fax: 61 3 9872 5454
salesenquiries@fortiori.com.au
www.fortiori.com.au

order direct on (03) 9872 3855

This publication is copyright. No part may be reproduced, stored in a retrieval system or transmitted in any form or by any means whether electronic, mechanical, photocopied, recorded or otherwise without the prior written permission of the publisher. Australian distribution to newsagents and supermarkets by Gordon and Gotch Ltd, 68 Kingsgrove Road, Belmore, NSW 2192.

Reprinted in 2004 by Toppan Printing Co (HK) Ltd.
Reprinted in 2005 by Toppan Printing Co (HK) Ltd.

ISBN 090 958 1609 2 9

DISCLAIMER: The nutritional information listed under each recipe does not include the nutrient content of garnishes or any accompaniments not listed in specific quantities in the ingredient list. The nutritional information for each recipe is an estimate only, and may vary depending on the brand of ingredients used, and due to natural biological variations in the composition of natural foods such as meat, fish, fruit and vegetables. The nutritional information was calculated by a qualified dietitian using FoodWorks dietary analysis software (Version 3, Xyris Software Pty Ltd, Highgate Hill, Queensland, Australia) based on the Australian food composition tables and food manufacturers' data. Where not specified, ingredients are always analysed as average or medium, not small or large. All recipes were analysed using 59 g eggs.

IMPORTANT: Those who might be at risk from the effects of salmonella food poisoning (the elderly, pregnant women, young children and those suffering from immune deficiency diseases) should consult their general practitioner about consuming raw or undercooked eggs.